STREET SECRETS

Brian Ward and Andrew Macdonald

Kingfisher Books

Educational advisers: Mary Jane Drummond,
Cambridge Institute of Education, Cambridge
Iris Walkinshaw, Headteacher, Rushmore Infants School, London

The author and publishers are grateful to the following
organizations for their technical advice in the preparation
of this book: Thames Water, Wessex Water, British Telecom,
The Electricity Council, British Gas, Westminster City Council
and London Underground Ltd. They would also like to thank the
many individuals who gave valuable help to the illustrator on site.

Kingfisher Books, Grisewood & Dempsey Ltd,
Elsley House, 24–30 Great Titchfield Street,
London W1P 7AD

This reformatted edition first published in 1992
by Kingfisher Books
10 9 8 7 6 5 4 3 2 1

Originally published in 1988 as *Stepping Stones 456: Under the Street*
by Kingfisher Books

© Grisewood & Dempsey Ltd 1988, 1992

All rights reserved. No part of this publication may
be reproduced, stored in a retrieval system or transmitted
by any means, electronic, mechanical, photocopying
or otherwise, without the prior permission of the publisher.

British Library Cataloguing in Publication Data
A catalogue record for this book is available
from the British Library.

ISBN 0 86272 954 8

Edited by Vanessa Clarke
Editorial assistant: Camilla Hallinan
Designed by Nick Cannan
Cover designed by Pinpoint Design Company
Phototypeset by Southern Positives and Negatives (SPAN),
Lingfield, Surrey
Printed and bound in Portugal

Contents

A Burst Pipe	4	Filling In the Road	20
Water Pipes	8	Going Underground	23
Drains and Sewers	9	Underground Railways	24
Storm-water Drains	12	In the Tunnel	26
Telephone Wires	14	Working Underground	28
Electricity Cables	16	Covers and Clues	30
Gas Pipes	18	Index	32

A Burst Pipe

Have you ever played games on the covers in the pavement? Interesting things are happening under each one. But we can't usually see what they are unless something goes wrong.

These repair workers have dug a hole to get at a water pipe which has cracked. They turn off the water while they dig and then turn it on for a moment to find out where the leak is. The pipe is a water main.

A worker shuts off the water in the main pipe by turning the main stop-valve with a long key. The valve is hidden under a metal lid in the road. The workers have brought a pump with them, and it sucks the muddy water out of the hole around the pipe.

The main stop-valve

The pump

The workers decide that the best way to repair this leak is to fit a metal collar tightly around the crack. They clean off the mud and fix on the metal collar with nuts and bolts. Then they turn on the water again at the stop-valve to make sure that the leak is sealed.

The metal collar

Water Pipes

The big water mains bring drinking water into the city from water treatment works and reservoirs.

In every street in the city there are small metal covers in the pavement. They cover the outside stop-valves in the water pipes going from the water main into buildings. Smaller pipes inside the buildings carry the water to taps for drinking, cooking and washing.

Drains and Sewers

Whenever you clean your teeth and wash your hands, the dirty water goes down the plughole into drain pipes. Lots more water is used for flushing the toilet and for baths, showers and washing machines. All this dirty water is carried away along the drain pipes into the sewer pipe. The sewer under the street has to be very large because all the dirty water from the buildings in the street pours into it.

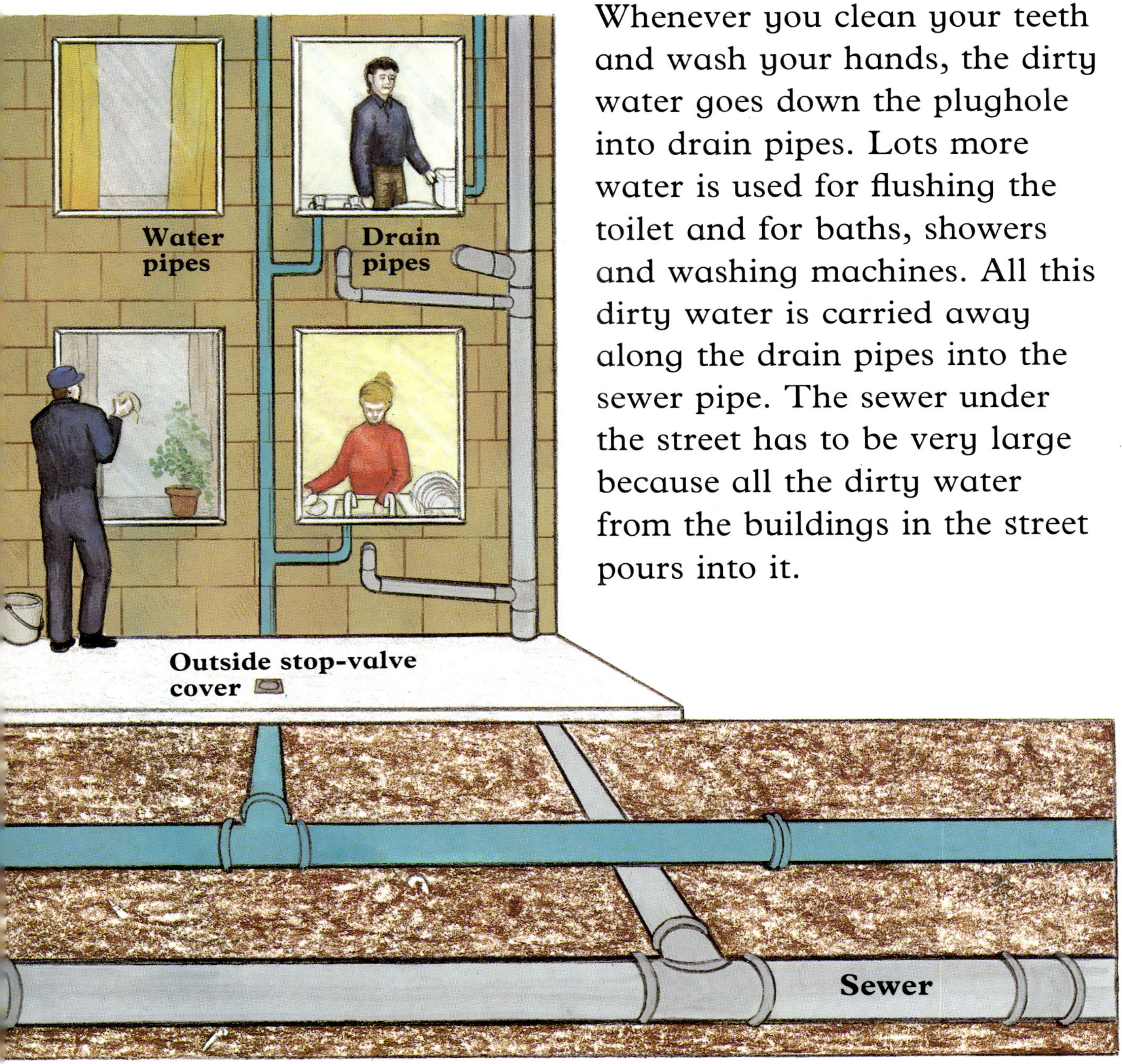

Eventually the smaller sewers from every street join the main sewer. This main sewer under the city is so big that it looks like a tunnel. The dirty water, called sewage, rushes along like a river to the sewage works where it will be cleaned.

Sewage inspectors can get into the sewer through heavy iron plates in the road. The ladder down to the sewer and the paths by the side of the sewer are damp and slippery so the inspectors must take great care. They wear protective clothing too.

Storm-water Drains

Up on the street again, rain-water is rushing along the gutter at the side of the road and gurgling down a drain. The storm-water drains carry the rain-water into pipes under the street so that the road is not flooded. Sometimes the pipes carry the rain-water into streams and rivers. Sometimes they carry it to water treatment works inside the city.

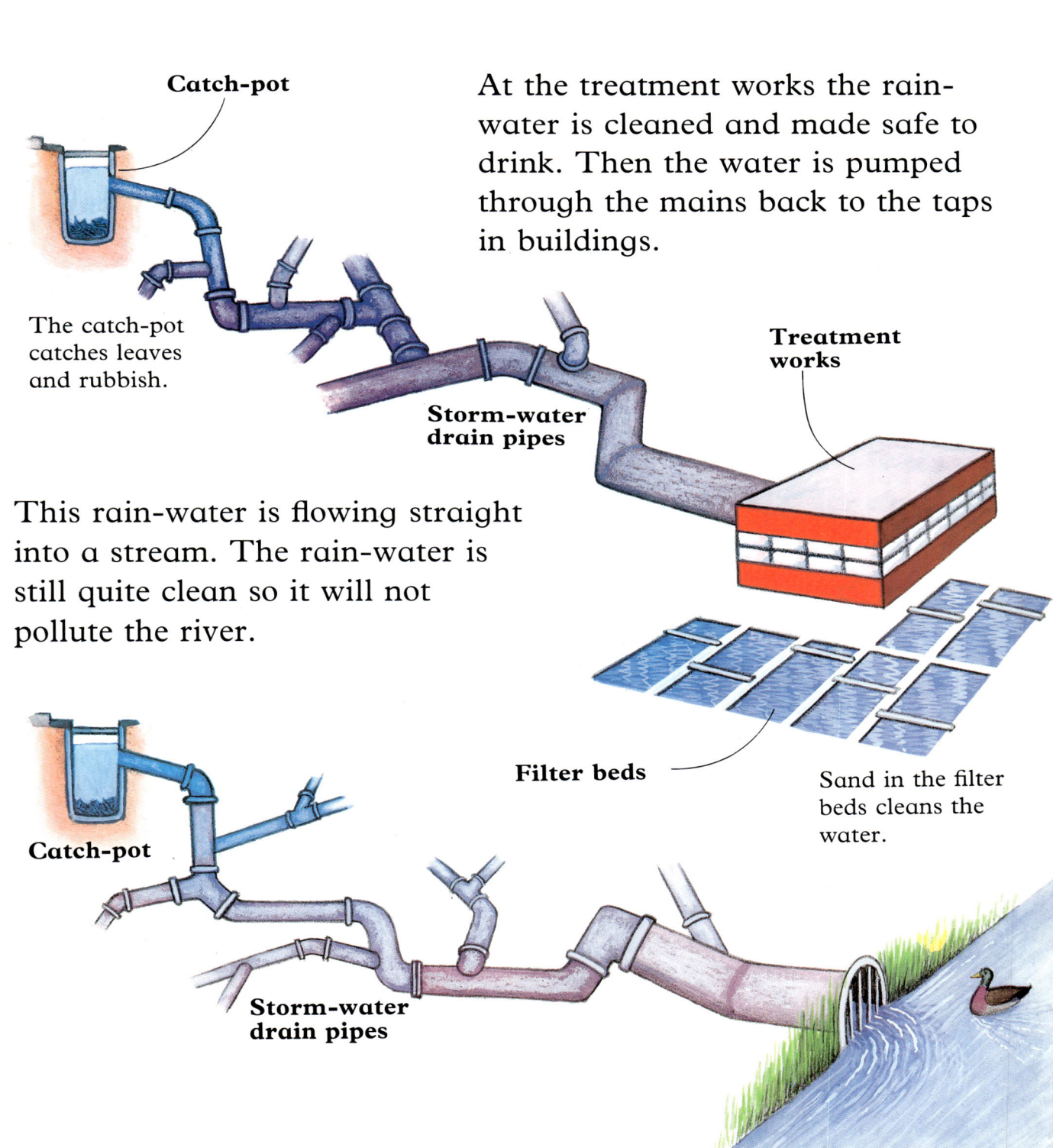

Catch-pot

The catch-pot catches leaves and rubbish.

At the treatment works the rain-water is cleaned and made safe to drink. Then the water is pumped through the mains back to the taps in buildings.

Storm-water drain pipes

Treatment works

This rain-water is flowing straight into a stream. The rain-water is still quite clean so it will not pollute the river.

Filter beds

Sand in the filter beds cleans the water.

Catch-pot

Storm-water drain pipes

Telephone Wires

Tiny metal wires connect our telephones, and these wires are inside cables under the street. Hundreds of copper wires are wrapped together in paper and plastic to make one thick cable. But the cables are easily

damaged so they are laid inside plastic pipes called trunking to protect them.

Footway box cover

These telephone engineers are replacing a section of cable between two footway boxes. They join the cable wires and make sure that they work by sending an electric signal along each one. They listen for the signal on their earphones.

The telephone engineers reach the cables by lifting lids in the pavement.

Footway box cover

Electricity Cables

Deeper down in the earth are the electricity cables that supply power to homes, shops and offices.

An electricity engineer is lifting the cover of a link box to inspect the fuses and cables. Metal wires inside the cable carry the electricity. They make heat so they are covered either with oil-paper or with plastic. Then they are sealed in metal and covered again, sometimes with tarred cloth, sometimes with plastic. The final cover protects the cables from damp and damage by workers digging up the pavement.

Gas Pipes

Gas comes into our homes along pipes under the ground. Old gas pipes were made of cast-iron and steel and look like water pipes but most new pipes are made of bright yellow plastic which is very strong and long-lasting.

Gas mains carry gas along the road and smaller pipes take the gas from the main to each home.

Gas at home

The Mole

Workers lay the pipes in different ways. Sometimes they can push a new pipe inside an old one. Sometimes they can use a tunnelling machine called a Mole to burrow a tunnel under the ground. Then they push a pipe through behind it. At other times, workers need to dig a trench in the road and lay the pipe inside. After all the pipes have been connected, the engineers test them to make sure that there are no leaks. Then they let the gas through.

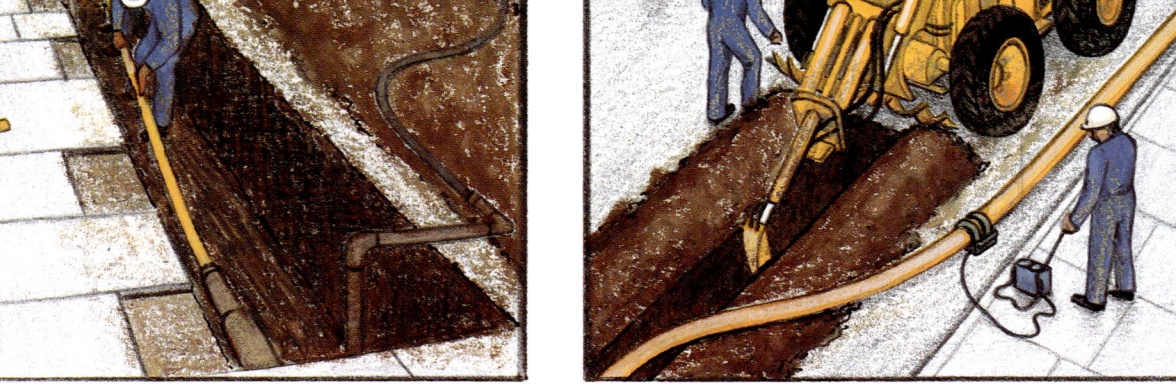

Pushing through new pipes    Digging a trench

Filling In the Road

After new pipes are laid and repairs are finished, the workers have to fill in the holes and make the road safe to drive on.

First they pack sand around pipes to protect them. Then they shovel in earth and crushed rock called hardcore, and ram it down with a compactor. Another worker heaps hot black asphalt on top. Finally a roller flattens the surface.

Now the road is smooth enough and strong enough to take the weight of cars, buses and lorries again.

Foundations

Going Underground

In a busy city, the space under the street is a useful place to tuck away all the pipes and cables. They are out of the way down there and we can't see them but they are busy supplying us with all the things we need every day.

Business people also make use of the space under the street for offices, storage space and car parks. Strong foundations go deep below the surface to support the weight of these buildings.

Tunnels called subways go under the street so that people can avoid the traffic on the busy road and cross in safety.

Subway

Underground Railways

Even further down under the street are the underground railways which carry people quickly around the city. Stairs and escalators go down from the ticket hall to the platforms where trains stop for passengers.

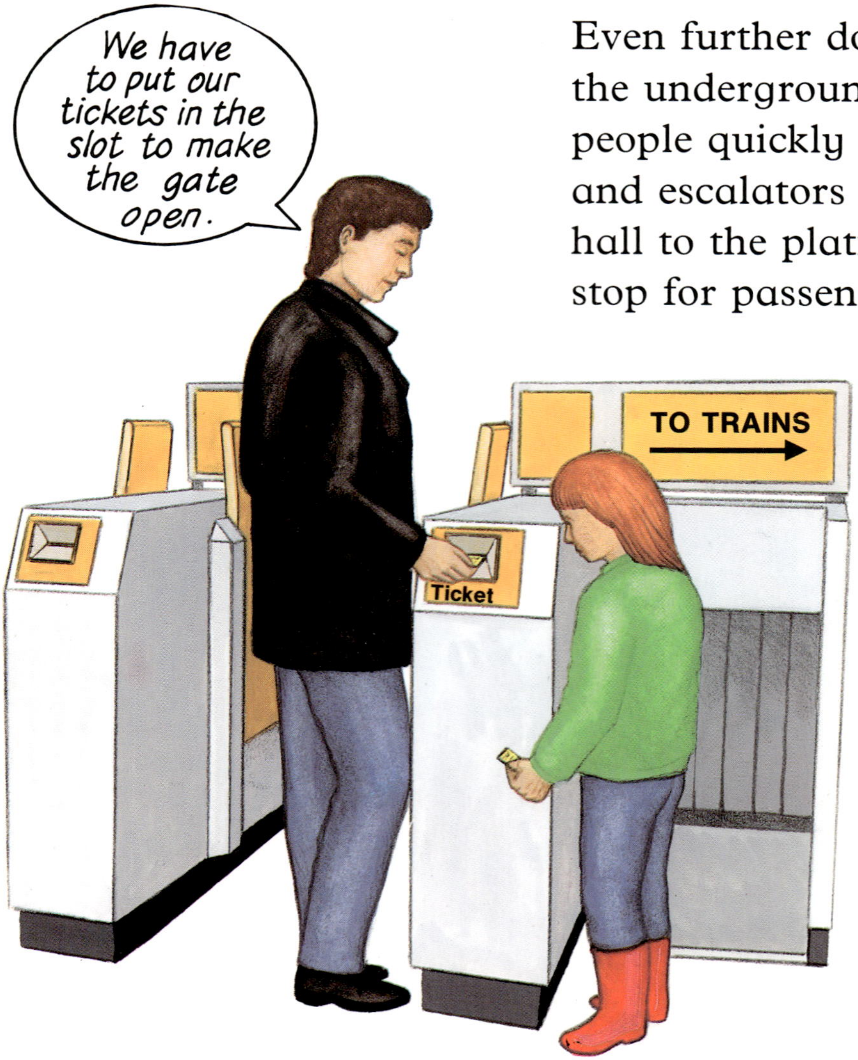

We have to put our tickets in the slot to make the gate open.
TO TRAINS
Ticket

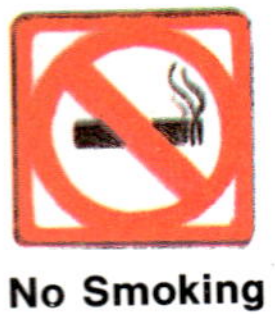

No Smoking

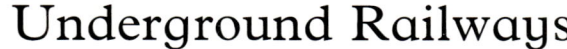

Trains travel on different lines under the city and each line has its own tunnels going from station to station under the ground.

In the Tunnel

All the tunnels in the station and under the street are round because a round shape is stronger than a square and a rectangular one. The round tunnels are lined with sheets of metal.

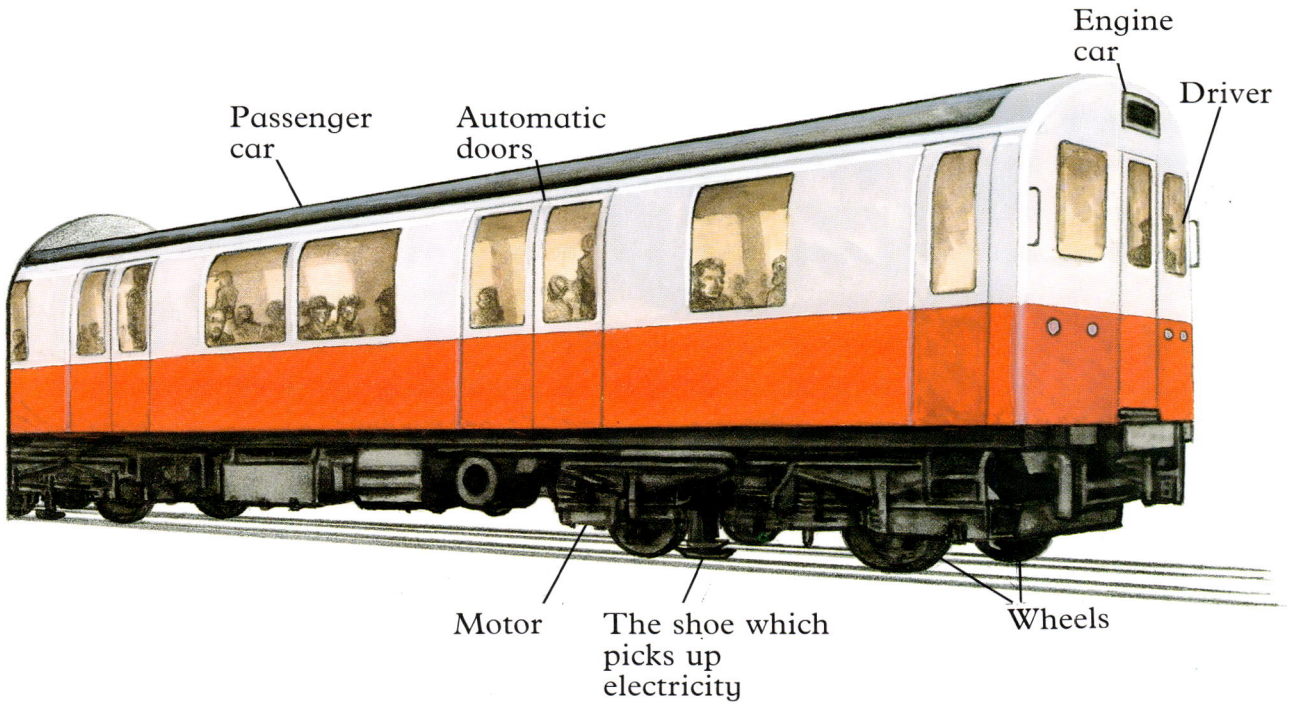

The underground trains look different from ordinary ones because they are shaped to fit the tunnels. The train is powered by a motor which picks up electricity from an electrified rail in the track. The driver controls the train, and watches for the signals telling her when to stop and start the train.

Working Underground

Many people work on the underground railways below the street.

Here are some of the people you see when you go on a train.

Covers and Clues

Up on the street again, the workers have gone and the children are jumping, skipping and hopping over the covers and lids in the pavement.

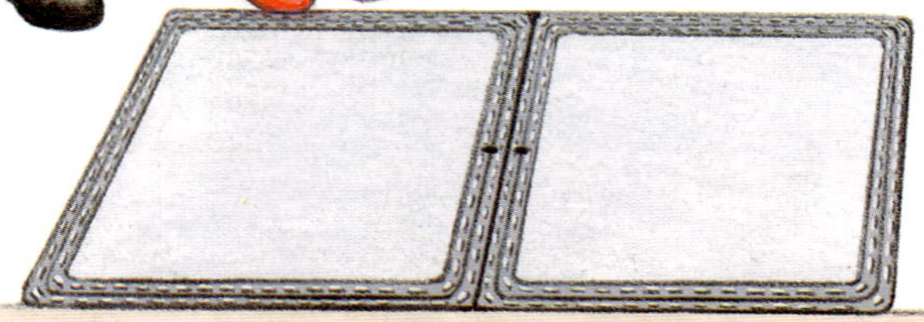

Telephone footway box cover

Outside water pipe stop-valve covers

Sewer inspection cover

Maybe you have played on them too. Some covers are made of metal; some are made of concrete; and some are made of plastic. Each type is a clue to the busy world hidden under the street.

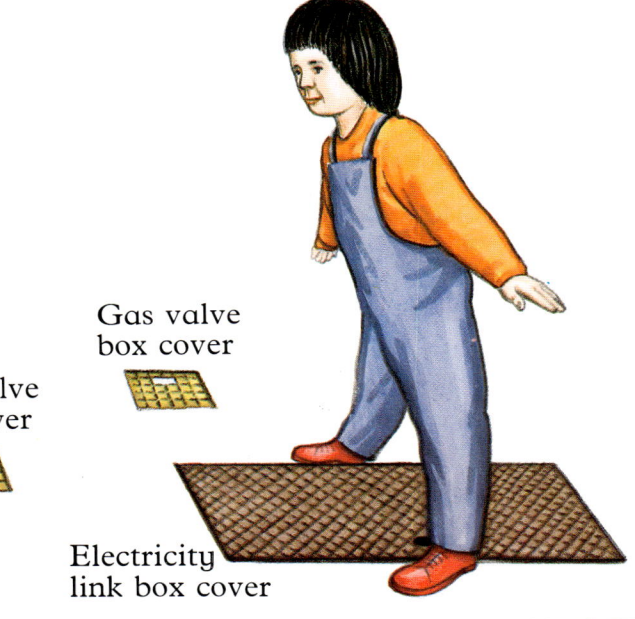

Gas valve box cover

Gas valve box cover

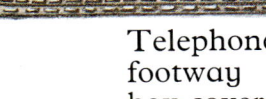

Telephone footway box cover

Electricity link box cover

Storm-water drain

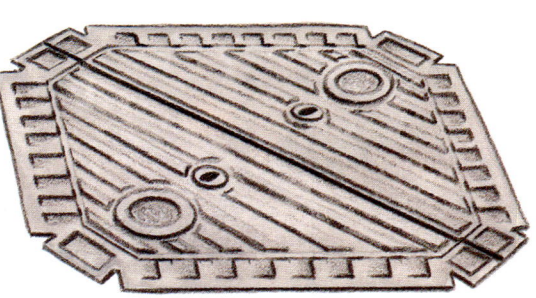

Water main inspection cover

Index

asphalt 20, 21

cables 14, 15, 16, 17, 21, 23
catch-pot 13
cleaner 29
compactor 20
controller 29
covers 5, 8, 14, 15, 16, 30, 31

drain pipes 8, 9
drains 12, 13

earth 16, 20
electricity 16, 17, 27
electricity cables 16, 17, 21, 23
electricity engineer 16, 17
escalators 24, 25

filter beds 13
foundations 22, 23

gas engineers 19
gas mains 18, 20
gas pipes 18, 19, 20, 23
gutters 12

hardcore 20

key 6

leaks 5, 7, 19
lids 6, 15, 30, 31

maintenance engineers 29
mole 19

platform guard 28
pollution 13
pump 6

rain-water 12, 13
repair workers 5, 6, 7
reservoirs 8, 13
rivers 10, 12
rock 20
roller 20, 21

sand 13, 20
sewage 10
sewage inspectors 11
sewage works 10
sewers 9, 10, 11, 23
sewer pipes 8, 9
stop-valves 5, 6, 7, 8, 30
storm-water drains 12, 13, 21, 23, 31
streams 12, 13
subway 22, 23

taps 8, 13
telephone cables 14, 15, 16, 21, 23

telephone engineers 15
telephones 14, 15
ticket inspector 28
train driver 27, 28
trunking 14
tunnelling machine 19
tunnels 10, 23, 24, 25, 27

underground railways 24–29
underground trains 24, 25, 26, 27, 28

water 5, 6, 7, 8, 9, 10, 13
water mains 4, 5, 6, 8, 13, 20
water pipes 5, 6, 8, 9, 13, 18, 23
water treatment works 8, 12, 13
wires 14, 15, 16